W9-BXZ-370

WORLD ALMANAC® LIBRARY OF THE STATES

Georgia

THE PEACH STATE

by Eric Siegfried Holtz

Curriculum Consultant: Jean Craven,
Director of Instructional Support,
Albuquerque, NM, Public Schools

WORLD ALMANAC® LIBRARY

Please visit our web site at: www.worldalmanaclibrary.com
For a free color catalog describing World Almanac® Library's
list of high-quality books and multimedia programs, call
1-800-848-2928 (USA) or 1-800-387-3178 (Canada).
World Almanac® Library's fax: (414) 332-3567.

Library of Congress Cataloging-in-Publication Data

Holtz, Eric Siegfried.
    Georgia, Empire State of the South / by Eric Siegfried Holtz.
       p. cm. — (World Almanac Library of the states)
    Includes bibliographical references and index.
    Summary: Illustrations and text present the history, geography, people, politics and
government, economy, and social life and customs of Georgia.
    ISBN 0-8368-5132-3 (lib. bdg.)
    ISBN 0-8368-5302-4 (softcover)
    1. Georgia—Juvenile literature. [1. Georgia.] I. Title. II. Series.
F286.3.H65   2002
975.8—dc21   2002022706

This edition first published in 2002 by
World Almanac® Library
330 West Olive Street, Suite 100
Milwaukee, WI 53212 USA

This edition © 2002 by World Almanac® Library.

Design and Editorial: Bill SMITH STUDIO Inc.
Editor: Kristen Behrens
Assistant Editor: Megan Elias
Art Director: Jay Jaffe
Photo Research: Sean Livingstone
World Almanac® Library Editors: Patricia Lantier, Monica Rausch
World Almanac® Library Production: Scott M. Krall, Tammy Gruenewald,
  Katherine A. Goedheer

Photo credits: p. 4 © Corbis; p. 6 (all) © Corel; p. 7 (top) © TimePix, (bottom) courtesy of the
Coca-Cola Company; p. 8 © Raymond Gehman; p. 10 © Ed Lallo/TimePix; p. 11 © Dover
Publications; p. 12 © Corbis; p. 13 © Library of Congress; p. 14 courtesy of Lockheed Martin
Aeronautics Company; p. 15 © Donald Uhrbrock/TimePix; p. 17 courtesy of Macon Georgia CVB;
p. 18 © PhotoDisc; p. 19 courtesy of Macon Georgia CVB; p. 20 (left to right) © ArtToday, courtesy
of Augusta, GA CVB, © Corel, © Christie K. Silver, © ArtToday, © ArtToday; p. 23 courtesy of
Columbus, GA CVB; p. 26 © Library of Congress; p. 27 courtesy of Augusta CVB; p. 29 © Library
of Congress; p. 31 (all) © Library of Congress; p. 32 courtesy of Macon CVB; p. 33 courtesy of
Athens, GA CVB; p. 34 © Corel; p. 35 courtesy of Columbus CVB; p. 36 courtesy of Macon CVB;
p. 37 (top) © Library of Congress, (bottom) © Bettmann/CORBIS; p. 38 © Dover Publications; p. 39
(top) © Dover Publications, (bottom) © PhotoDisc; p. 40 (top) © PhotoDisc, (bottom) © Library of
Congress; p. 42–43 © Library of Congress; p. 44 (top) © PhotoDisc, (bottom) © PhotoSpin; p. 45
(top) © PhotoSpin, (bottom) courtesy of Columbus CVB

Printed in the United States of America

1 2 3 4 5 6 7 8 9 06 05 04 03 02

Georgia

Dream of Georgia

Georgia is a state of hopes and dreams. The colony of Georgia was founded on Englishman James Oglethorpe's vision of giving the poor of Great Britain a second chance. In the years before the Revolutionary War, Georgia prospered, and many Georgians fulfilled their hopes of wealth.

Georgia joined in the struggle for freedom from Great Britain and became the fourth state to ratify the U.S. Constitution in 1788. Thousands of settlers arrived in Georgia in the early years of the republic, driven by dreams of sharing the state's economic prosperity. Much of that wealth, however, was created by a system that depended on slave labor, and by the mid-1800s, the winds of change were threatening that system.

The Civil War and its aftermath had a devastating effect on much of Georgia. Aspirations for a better way of life led many Georgians to leave and join the Great Migration to the cities of the north, such as Detroit and Chicago. Atlanta prospered, however, and became one of the most important cities in the south, serving as a transportation hub for the region.

The beauty and hopeful spirit of this state has inspired Georgians to achieve in many areas. After World War II, the hopes and dreams of African Americans in Georgia drew national attention as the Civil Rights Movement gathered strength. One of the state's most famous sons, Dr. Martin Luther King, Jr., shared his vision of peace and equality with the world in his famous "I have a dream" speech. The work of Dr. King and other Georgians, such as Julian Bond, who served in the Georgia House of Representatives, and Coretta Scott King, who continues to be a voice for racial harmony, led to enormous changes in U.S. society. During the last decades of the twentieth century, Georgia's economy began to flourish, as practical dreamers such as media giant Ted Turner and the executives of CNN, United Parcel Service, and Delta Air Lines established thriving businesses in the state.

▶ Map of Georgia showing the interstate highway system, as well as major cities and waterways.

▼ Peaches ripening in the Georgia sun.

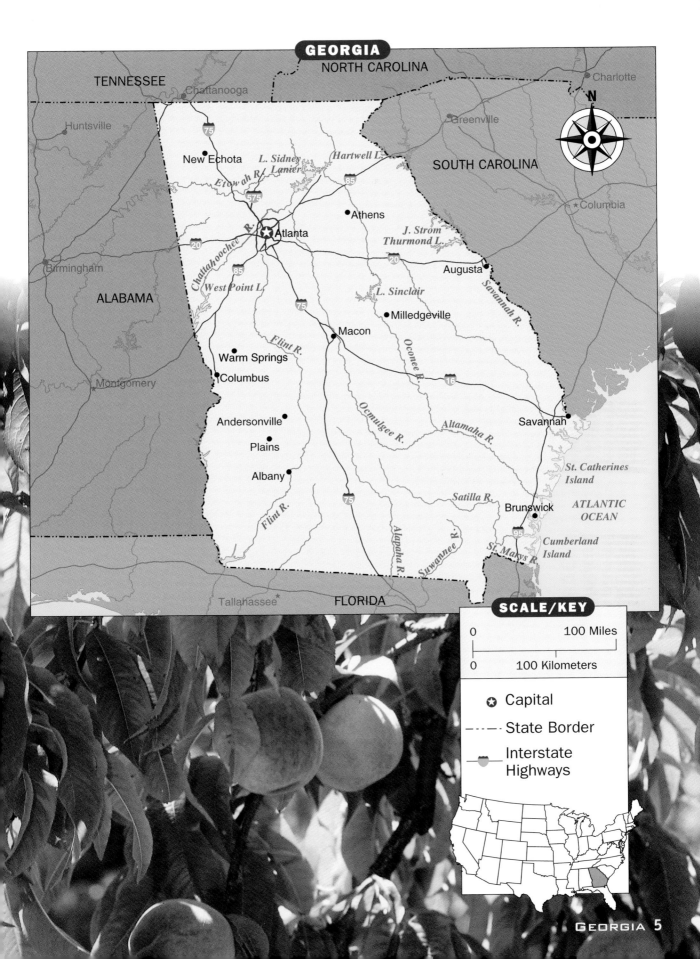

TENNESSEE

NORTH CAROLINA

Chattanooga

Charlotte

Huntsville

N

Greenville

SOUTH CAROLINA

New Echota

L. Sidney Lanier

Hartwell L.

Etowah R.

Columbia

Athens

Atlanta

J. Strom Thurmond L.

Birmingham

ALABAMA

Chattahoochee R.

West Point L.

L. Sinclair

Augusta

Savannah R.

Milledgeville

Macon

Oconee R.

Warm Springs

Flint R.

Columbus

Montgomery

Andersonville

Ocmulgee R.

Altamaha R.

Savannah

Plains

Albany

St. Catherines Island

Satilla R.

ATLANTIC OCEAN

Flint R.

Brunswick

Suwannee R.

Alapaha R.

Cumberland Island

St. Marys R.

Tallahassee

FLORIDA

SCALE/KEY

0   100 Miles

0   100 Kilometers

⊗ Capital

---·--- State Border

🛡 Interstate Highways

Fast Facts

GEORGIA (GA), Peach State, Empire State of the South

Entered Union
January 2, 1788 (4th state)

Capital	Population
Atlanta	416,474

Total Population (2000)
8,186,453 (10th most populous state) — *Between 1990 and 2000, the state's population increased 26.4 percent.*

Largest Cities	Population
Atlanta	416,474
Augusta-Richmond	199,775
Columbus	186,291
Savannah	131,510
Athens-Clarke	101,489

Land Area
57,906 square miles (149,976 square kilometers) (21st largest state)

State Motto
"Wisdom, Justice, and Moderation"

State Song
"Georgia on My Mind" *by Stuart Gorrell and Hoagy Carmichael*

State Bird
Brown thrasher — *Georgia's hockey team is called the Atlanta Thrashers.*

State Game Bird
Bobwhite quail

State Fish
Largemouth bass

State Butterfly
Tiger swallowtail

State Insect
Honeybee

State Marine Mammal
Right whale

State Flower
Cherokee rose

State Wildflower
Azalea

State Tree
Live oak

State Mineral
Staurolite — *Often called "fairy crosses" or "fairy stones," staurolite crystals are collected as good luck charms.*

State Crop
Peanut — *Georgia produces nearly half of the total United States peanut crop.*

State Fossil
Shark tooth

State Fruit
Peach

State Vegetable
Vidalia onion — *Vidalia onions are so sweet and delicious they can be eaten like apples. They grow in the fields of Vidalia and Glenville in southern Georgia.*

PLACES TO VISIT

Martin Luther King, Jr., National Historic Site, *Atlanta*
The site includes the grave of Dr. Martin Luther King, Jr., and exhibits that commemorate Dr. King's leading role in the Civil Rights Movement.

Ocmulgee National Monument, *Macon*
Impressive remains of the prehistoric Mound Builder civilization, as well as later Native American villages, are preserved here.

Stone Mountain Memorial Park, *Stone Mountain*
The park is 16 miles (26 kilometers) northeast of Atlanta. A huge carving on the face of Stone Mountain depicts three of the leaders of the Southern Confederacy — Jefferson Davis, Robert E. Lee, and Stonewall Jackson — on horseback.

For other places and events, see p. 44.

BIGGEST, BEST, AND MOST

- Fort Benning, near Columbus, is one of the largest Army camps in the country.

- Cumberland Island, Georgia's southernmost barrier island, is the largest undeveloped island on the Atlantic Coast.

- The Central State Hospital in Milledgeville has the world's largest kitchen. It can cook up to thirty thousand meals a day.

STATE FIRSTS

- **1828** The first gold rush in the United States occurred in Dahlonega.
- **1834** The first iron seagoing vessel was built in Savannah. It was called the *John Randolph*.
- **1866** Georgia became the first state to allow women full property rights.
- **1943** Georgia became the first state to allow eighteen-year-olds the right to vote.

Babyland

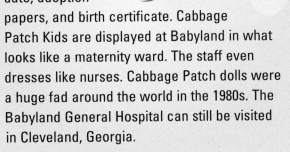

Thousands and thousands of "kids" have been "born" at Babyland General Hospital since 1982. Each "Cabbage Patch Kid" is unique, with its own name, birth date, adoption papers, and birth certificate. Cabbage Patch Kids are displayed at Babyland in what looks like a maternity ward. The staff even dresses like nurses. Cabbage Patch dolls were a huge fad around the world in the 1980s. The Babyland General Hospital can still be visited in Cleveland, Georgia.

The Life of Coke

Coca-Cola was invented in Atlanta, Georgia, in 1886. Dr. John S. Pemberton, a pharmacist, created the formula, but it was his bookkeeper and son-in-law, Frank Robinson, who came up with the name. Total sales for the first year were only $50. In 1919, the company was sold for $25 million. Today Coca-Cola is the world's most successful brand name, recognized by at least 90 percent of the world's population. The Coca-Cola Company is still based in Atlanta. Every second of every day, about seven thousand of Coke's soft drinks are consumed around the world. The first outdoor sign advertising Coca-Cola still exists. It was painted in 1894 and can be found in Cartersville, near Atlanta.

A State of Change

In America there are fertile Lands sufficient to subsist all the Poor in England, and distressed Protestants in Europe; yet Thousands starve for want of mere Sustenance.

— An Account of the Designs of the Trustees for establishing the Colony of Georgia in America, *1733*

By about 10,000 B.C., Paleo-Indians, the first people to inhabit North America, had settled throughout the continent, including what is now Georgia. They began as small groups of nomadic hunter-gatherers.

By the Mississippian period (A.D. 900–1550), permanent settlements were established. Most included a number of large mounds, which may have been used as bases for temples and other important buildings, as well as for burials. No one is really sure what happened to the Mississippian mound builders, but even before Europeans arrived, the towns had mostly been deserted. Georgia's history begins with that mystery. When the Europeans first arrived in 1521, there were about a dozen Native American groups in Georgia. The largest were the Cherokee (Keetoowha) and the Creek (Muskogee).

Native Americans of Georgia
Cherokee (Keetoowha)
Creek (Muskogee)
Savannah
Timucua
Westo
Yamacraw
Yamassee

Spanish Exploration and Settlement

The first Europeans to explore southeastern North America were from Spain. They reached Georgia twenty-nine years after Christopher Columbus landed in the Bahamas. At first the Spanish mainly sailed along the coastline. Then, beginning in 1540, Hernando de Soto led an overland expedition through land that would become Florida, Georgia, and beyond. Coastal settlements followed. Pedro Menendez de Aviles, a naval officer, founded a mission on Saint Catherines Island in 1566. A mission is a settlement designed to spread religion, in this case Roman Catholic Christianity by way of the Franciscan order. By the 1590s there were Franciscan missions along the Atlantic Coast from Florida to South Carolina, including the coast of *Guale,* the Spanish name for the Georgia area.

DID YOU KNOW?

Georgia has never really settled on a state nickname. Empire State of the South is just one of many options. Others include Peach State, Goober State, Cracker State, and Buzzard State.

Spain believed it had the right to govern Guale. France and England had established colonies in North America, and they disagreed. Their settlements squeezed Guale from the west and north. English settlers in the Carolinas pushed southward and attacked the Spanish missions. The Spanish were forced to give up Saint Catherines Island in 1680 and lost Guale almost completely by 1686.

The Georgia Colony

In 1732, the king of Great Britain, which included England, established a colony between the Savannah and Altamaha Rivers, claiming its borders extended west all the way to the Pacific Ocean. The king's name was George II, so the colony was called Georgia. The English wanted the colony to serve as a buffer between the territory they held in the Carolinas and Spain's holdings in Florida. James Oglethorpe, an English member of Parliament, and others became Georgia's "trustees." They wanted the colony to be a refuge for persecuted religious groups and the poor. In 1732, Oglethorpe sailed up the Savannah River and landed at Yamacraw Bluff, where he was welcomed by the Yamacraw people. About one hundred settlers returned with Oglethorpe on February 12, 1733, to establish Savannah. It survived to become the first permanent European settlement in Georgia. The early years of the colony, however, were perilous.

▼ The Great Temple Mound lies within the Etowah Indian Mounds State Historic Site along the Etowah River. The mound was built circa A.D. 950.

The biggest threat came in 1739 when the War of Jenkins' Ear broke out between Great Britain and Spain. The Spanish invaded Georgia in 1742 but were defeated at the Battle of Bloody Marsh, near Fort Frederica on the southern coast.

Oglethorpe wanted Georgia to be a model society. Slavery, strong liquor, and the buying and selling of large parcels of land were all prohibited. No other British colony in North America had laws such as these, and not everyone agreed with them. Some settlers argued that the colony would not flourish until they could own large estates and could use slaves as cheap labor. The trustees were eventually forced to make changes. By 1750, Georgia was more similar to the other colonies. Liquor was legalized, slavery became more widespread, and land deals led to larger and larger plantations. The trustees returned Georgia to the king in 1752. Two years later it officially became a royal colony.

Since Georgia's founding, Spain and England had disagreed over the colony's boundary with Spanish-controlled Florida. After the French and Indian War ended in 1763, the nations agreed that the colony's western border was the Mississippi River and the southern border St. Marys River. All land west of the Appalachians was reserved for Native

▼ **A map of Savannah circa 1734.**

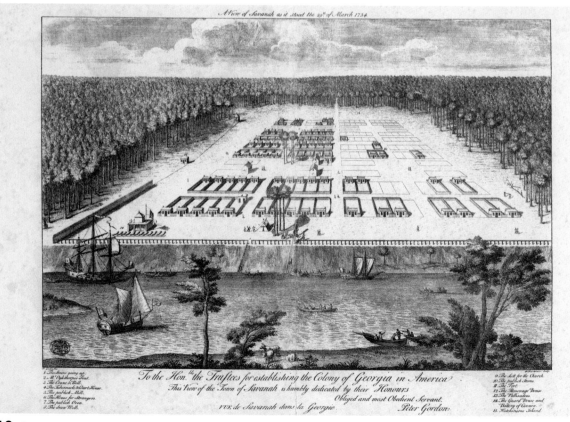

Americans, but European settlements soon began encroaching. Georgia's northwestern border eventually extended into this territory. The settler population grew rapidly, from only about five thousand in 1752 to about twenty-five thousand in 1776. At this time, there were also about twenty-five thousand slaves living in Georgia.

The War of Independence

Georgia prospered in the period prior to the Revolutionary War. The colony produced rice, indigo (used for dyeing textiles), pork, sugar (used to make rum), and maritime supplies for export to Britain and other colonies. The youngest and least populated American colony, it was also the least revolutionary, perhaps in part because it had to defend its southern border against Spanish forces. Georgia was the only one of the thirteen colonies that did not send delegates to the First Continental Congress in 1774. That congress debated resistance to British rule and issued a Declaration of Rights and Grievances. Colonial resistance hardened into battle in 1775. Georgia elected delegates to the Second Continental Congress in that same year. Lyman Hall, George Walton, and Button Gwinnett signed the Declaration of Independence for Georgia. The British captured Savannah in 1778 and soon reestablished control over most of Georgia. In 1779, colonial forces and their French allies failed in an attempt to take back Savannah. It was not until 1781 that the United States retook Augusta, and British troops did not leave Savannah until 1782. Independence was not easily won.

Early Statehood

On January 2, 1788, at a state convention meeting in Augusta, Georgia became the fourth state to ratify the U.S. Constitution. Georgia's continuing prosperity made it a land of opportunity for thousands of settlers arriving from other states. The state's population more than tripled in the twenty years between 1790 and 1810.

James Edward Oglethorpe

As a member of the British Parliament, James Oglethorpe was disturbed by the situation of his country's debtors. In those days, people in Britain were put in jail for owing money they could not pay. Since it was difficult for anyone to earn money to pay back debts while in jail, Oglethorpe wanted to give the debtors a break — in Georgia. The need for a buffer colony against the Spanish, however, was the main argument Oglethorpe used to convince the king to grant the colony. That was an effective strategy, and Oglethorpe's military skills — he defeated Spanish attempts to encroach on the colony's borders — were crucial to the early survival of Georgia. In the end, few debtors came, and many of Oglethorpe's other ideals for the colony were also frustrated. Despite his best efforts, slavery, alcohol, and social inequality were introduced.

Increase in settlement made land ever more precious. The United States and Britain again fought one another during the War of 1812. Georgia, in an attempt to gain more land for itself, used this war to attempt to extend its southern border farther into Florida, as well as to gain land currently held by Native Americans. Georgian forces twice attacked the Spanish in Florida, but without success. When the Creek took Britain's side against the United States, General John Floyd led a force of Georgia volunteers into the Creek territory of southwestern Georgia and defeated them there. The Upper Creek were also defeated in 1814 at the Battle of Horseshoe Bend in Alabama. The Creek were then forced to sign a treaty giving up much of their land. By 1827 they had lost all their lands in Georgia and moved west to Indian Territory, now the state of Oklahoma.

In northern Georgia the Cherokee had adopted many European ways. The Cherokee nation had a written constitution, and a newspaper, the *Cherokee Phoenix*, was printed in both Cherokee and English. Some rich Cherokee even owned African slaves. That all counted for little when gold was discovered on Cherokee lands in 1828. Gold prospectors moved in, and the Georgia government soon claimed the right to govern the area. In 1830, the federal Indian Removal Act offered Native Americans land in the

▼ Atlanta was a transportation hub in the South. General William T. Sherman targeted Georgia's railroads on his 1864 march. Here, part of a Confederate railroad system lies in ruins.

western prairie if they would leave their homes east of the Mississippi. An official land lottery was held in 1832 that handed out Cherokee lands to whites. In 1838 federal troops were sent to move the Cherokee to Indian Territory. More than eighteen thousand were forced to leave, and about four thousand died during the journey that became known as the "Trail of Tears."

The Civil War

After the invention of the cotton gin by Eli Whitney in Georgia in 1793, making it much easier to remove the seeds from the cotton fibers, cotton became the basis of Georgia's booming economy. Cotton was grown on plantations that depended on slave labor. By 1860 four out of every nine Georgians were slaves, yet there was increasing pressure from the Northern states to limit slavery. Many in the South felt they had a right to own slaves. Republican Abraham Lincoln, opposed to slavery, was elected president in 1860. South Carolina responded by seceding from (leaving) the Union in December 1860. Georgia opted for secession on January 19, 1861, joining other Southern states in the Confederate States of America. Although he opposed the decision to secede, U.S. Congressman from Georgia, Alexander Stephens, was chosen as vice president of the Confederacy.

The Civil War between the Union and the Confederacy began on April 12, 1861. In April 1862, Union forces captured Fort Pulaski, near the mouth of the Savannah River. The next year Georgia was the site of a major Confederate victory at the Battle of Chickamauga, in September 1863. In 1864 a Union army led by General William T. Sherman invaded Georgia. Sherman's army captured Atlanta in September and set it on fire in November. Sherman then began a "march to the sea." All along the way, everything of military or economic value was destroyed — an effective attempt to cripple the South's ability to support its troops and continue the war. Houses and fields were looted, bridges burned, railroad tracks torn up, and factories destroyed. Sherman reached Savannah in December and then turned northward into the Carolinas. A few months later, in April 1865, the Confederacy surrendered.

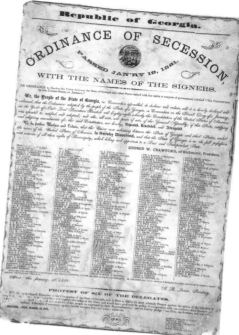

▲ Georgia's Ordinance of Secession was passed on January 19, 1861.

Worse Than War?

Andersonville, in southern Georgia, is among the most infamous sites of the Civil War. Officially known as Camp Sumter, Andersonville Prison was built early in 1864 when the Confederates decided to move Union prisoners farther away from the front lines of battle. Overcrowding, poor sanitation, and meager rations led to the deaths of almost thirteen thousand of the approximately forty-five thousand Union soldiers confined there.

Reconstruction

The period of Reconstruction after the Civil War was extremely difficult. The federal government had specific ideas about what kinds of laws the new state government should enact, which caused both resentment and resistance. Meanwhile the many battles that had taken place in Georgia resulted in a need to rebuild towns, cities, and railroads, although there were few funds available. Slavery was outlawed, but African Americans were far from receiving equal treatment. A system of racial segregation (separation) was developed, with facilities for African Americans always inferior to those for whites. Some whites even joined violent racist groups such as the Ku Klux Klan. The large plantations that once depended on slave labor were divided into smaller farms operated by tenant farmers or sharecroppers.

In 1910 half of all white farmers and 87 percent of African-American farmers did not own their own farms, giving them little incentive to develop the land. The state's great dependence on cotton left it devastated by the boll weevil, an insect that came to the state in 1913 and destroyed most of the cotton crop in the early 1920s. In what is known as the Great Migration, thousands of desperately poor people abandoned farms and moved to cities, often in states farther north. Worse was yet to come.

The stock market crash of 1929 led to the Great Depression of the 1930s. Georgia, along with the South as a whole, seemed to fall further and further behind the rest of the country. Georgia was among the very poorest states for nearly a century after the Civil War. One bright spot, however, was the booming railroad city of Atlanta.

Revival

World War II was the beginning of better economic times for Georgia. Federal money in support of the war effort poured into the state's industries and military bases, stimulating an economic revival that continues today. There was also great social and political change, especially

▲ Lockheed, today known as Lockheed-Martin, was one of the large-scale manufacturing firms that helped Georgia to industrialize in the twentieth century. Lockheed made the C-5A for the U.S. Air Force in 1969. The plane can be refueled in mid-air.

DID YOU KNOW?

Georgia has a "Little White House." It was built for the United States's thirty-second president, Franklin Delano Roosevelt, who visited Warm Springs so many times he considered it his second home. He died there on April 12, 1945.

in race relations. African-American soldiers returning from World War II demanded change. Atlanta, the home of Dr. Martin Luther King, Jr., was a center of the Civil Rights Movement, which sought an end to racial segregation and discrimination. A court case in 1954 gave the movement new legal momentum. In *Brown v. Board of Education,* the U.S. Supreme Court decided that segregated schools were not allowed by the Constitution. Public schools and colleges were slowly forced to integrate. The state's changes were highlighted in the 1970s by the election of Jimmy Carter, first as Georgia's governor, then as the nation's president. In his inaugural speech as governor, Carter urged Georgians to realize that "the time for racial discrimination is over."

In the last decades of the twentieth century, Georgia made further strides, especially economically. Georgia has recently been growing much more rapidly than the nation as a whole. Reversing a long historical trend, many more people are moving to the state than are moving away. Personal income is drawing even with the rest of the country, and the metropolitan Atlanta region is wealthier than the national average.

M. L. K.

Dr. Martin Luther King, Jr., was a native of Atlanta. He became a leader of the Civil Rights Movement, which sought equal treatment for all races. His powerful speeches and peaceful protests brought great change to U.S. society. His Alabama protest march from Selma to Montgomery, for example, helped bring about the Voting Rights Act of 1965. Dr. King was arrested thirty times for participating in civil rights protests, drawing worldwide attention. In 1964 he received the Nobel Peace Prize. The world was horrified when Dr. King was shot and killed by James Earl Ray in 1968.

Below: Dr. Martin Luther King, Jr., is released from an Albany, Georgia, jail after having been arrested for a civil rights protest.

Growing Georgia

> There shall be liberty of conscience allowed in the Worship of God to all persons inhabiting... our said Province. And that all persons Except Papists [Catholics] shall have a Free Exercise of their Religion.
> — *Georgia Charter, 1732*

From 1990 to 2000, Georgia's population grew by more than 26 percent. That is twice the rate for the United States as a whole. Growth is far from even, however. Nearly half of the population lives in and around Atlanta, while the other half is distributed throughout all the rest of the state. Atlanta functions not only as Georgia's capital city, but also as a commercial, transportation, and communication hub for the entire southeastern United States. In addition to the original central business district, the Atlanta area now contains three suburban centers, each about the size of a small city. Some of the world's largest corporations have their headquarters in the skyscrapers that make up Atlanta's modern skyline.

Savannah is the state's oldest city and a major seaport. Its relatively slow growth has allowed it to keep much of its

Age Distribution in Georgia
(2000 Census)

0–4	595,150
5–19	1,819,620
20–24	592,196
25–44	2,652,764
45–64	1,741,448
65 & over	785,275

Patterns of Immigration

The total number of people who immigrated to Georgia in 1998 was 10,445. Of that number, the largest immigrant groups were from Mexico (15.6%), India (8.4%), and Vietnam (5.7%).

Across One Hundred Years

Georgia's three largest foreign-born groups for 1890 and 1990

■ 1890   ■ 1990

Germany	Ireland	England	Mexico	Germany	Korea
3,679	3,374	1,585	20,309	13,268	11,678

Total state population: 1,837,353
Total foreign-born: 12,137 (1%)

Total state population: 6,478,216
Total foreign-born: 173,126 (3%)

old Southern charm, attracting increasing numbers of tourists from around the world. Other major cities include Columbus, Macon, Albany, and Augusta. It was not until 1960 that people in Georgia's urban areas outnumbered those in its rural areas. By 1990 urban dwellers were already 63 percent of the state's population.

Ethnicities

At first most Europeans immigrating to Georgia settled along the coast. The first permanent settlers came mainly from England, but there were also significant numbers of Germanic settlers. Northern Georgia was settled later, initially by people of Scottish and Irish descent who arrived from states to the north. In 2000, the descendants of Europeans made up about 65 percent of the population. The majority of them are of northern European descent.

At the time of the Civil War, nearly half of the state's population were African Americans. Most were slaves who gained their freedom through the Emancipation Proclamation of 1863. Freedom, however, came with few opportunities for advancement in Georgia. African Americans moved away in large numbers to cities in

▲ Dancing is a big part of the Ocmulgee Indian Celebration in Macon.

DID YOU KNOW?

The number of people in Georgia more than sixty-five years old is growing twice as fast as the number of people under sixty-five. Georgians are living longer, and people also are retiring to Georgia from other — colder — states.

Heritage and Background, Georgia   Year 2000

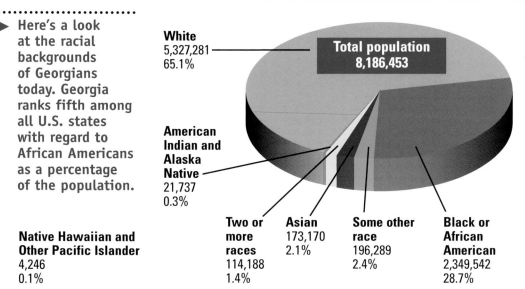

▶ Here's a look at the racial backgrounds of Georgians today. Georgia ranks fifth among all U.S. states with regard to African Americans as a percentage of the population.

White
5,327,281
65.1%

Total population
8,186,453

American Indian and Alaska Native
21,737
0.3%

Native Hawaiian and Other Pacific Islander
4,246
0.1%

Two or more races
114,188
1.4%

Asian
173,170
2.1%

Some other race
196,289
2.4%

Black or African American
2,349,542
28.7%

Note: 5.3% (435,227) of the population identify themselves as **Hispanic** or **Latino,** a cultural designation that crosses racial lines. Hispanics and Latinos are counted in this category as well as the racial category of their choice.

other states, and Georgia's African-American population declined to about 25 percent. Desegregation and better economic conditions have recently turned things around. The percentage of African Americans in the state is now increasing. In 2000, African Americans made up 28.7 percent of the overall population. Many of the larger cities have a greater proportion of African-American residents. In Savannah, African Americans are more than half the population, while in Atlanta they make up nearly two-thirds.

Hispanics and Asians are two ethnic groups that are growing rapidly. Native Americans have been only a small proportion of the population since the major groups, the Creek and the Cherokee, were driven out of the state early in the nineteenth century.

Educational Levels of Georgia Workers (age 25 and over)

Less than 9th grade	483,755
9th to 12th grade, no diploma	686,060
High school graduate, including equivalency	1,192,935
Some college, no degree or associate degree	883,512
Bachelor's degree	519,613
Graduate or professional degree	257,545

▼ The skyline of Atlanta, Georgia's capital and largest city.

Penta Hotel

Religion

Most Georgians are of Protestant Christian faiths. That is because the colony's founders provided refuge for Protestants fleeing religious discrimination in Europe. The Church of England was organized as early as 1733 in Savannah. Scottish Presbyterians and several kinds of German Protestants were also major forces early in Georgia's history. A small group of Jews has been present in the state almost from the beginning. Roman Catholics, who were at first excluded from the Georgia colony, did not found a permanent church in Georgia until late in the eighteenth century. (The early Catholic missions established by the Spanish should not be forgotten, but they did not become permanent.) A Baptist church was first organized in 1772 and attracted many devotees. Baptists now make up more than half of Georgia's churchgoers. Methodism became a major force in the state in the late eighteenth century and is now the second largest religious group in Georgia.

Education

The Georgia state constitution of 1777 planned for public schools in each county. Because the state lacked funds, however, public elementary schools were not state-financed until 1872 and public high schools until 1912. School attendance is compulsory for Georgians aged seven to sixteen. More than 7 percent of Georgia students attend private schools.

There are more than one hundred institutions of higher learning in Georgia. This includes the thirty-four campuses of the University System of Georgia.

Georgia also has some excellent private colleges and universities. A group of historically African-American institutions in Atlanta is known as the Atlanta University Center. It includes the Interdenominational Theological Center, Clark Atlanta University, Morehouse College, Morehouse School of Medicine, Spelman College, and Morris Brown College. Other notable private institutions include Emory University and Mercer University.

▲ Young Georgians enjoy the Tubman African American Museum in Macon.

Ja La Gee Means "Cherokee"

Cherokee leader Sequoya saw that a written language contributed to the whites' power, so he invented one for his people. It took twelve years, but in 1821 he completed a system of symbols that represented every sound in the Cherokee language. Sequoya's system was a major breakthrough. Within a few years, a Cherokee newspaper was published and a constitution was written for the Cherokee nation. The writing system is still used today by the approximately ten thousand Cherokee speakers in Oklahoma and North Carolina.

Plains and Plateaus

> I think it is the pleasantest climate in the world; for it is neither too warm in the summer, nor too cold in the winter. They certainly have the finest water in the world, and the land is extra-ordinary good.
>
> — *Anonymous, "A New Voyage to Georgia," 1730s*

Georgia is the largest state (in land area) east of the Mississippi. Its total land area is 57,906 square miles (149,976 sq km). It can be divided into six natural regions: the Atlantic Coastal Plain, the Gulf Coastal Plain, the Piedmont Plateau, the Blue Ridge Province, the Ridge and Valley Province, and the Appalachian Plateaus.

Highest Point

Brasstown Bald Mountain
4,784 feet (1,458 m) above sea level

The Coastal Plains

The Atlantic Coastal Plain and Gulf Coastal Plain together occupy about 60 percent of Georgia. The main difference between them is that rivers in the Atlantic Coastal Plain mostly flow eastward to the Atlantic Ocean, while in the Gulf Coastal Plain they flow southward to the Gulf of Mexico. The coastal plains are generally flat, although farther to the north are some hills. Salt marshes, which flood with seawater at high tide, are found along the Atlantic coast. Farther inland there are many freshwater swamps. The huge Okefenokee Swamp is in the southeastern part of the state along the border of both coastal plains. It is the largest swamp in North America

▼ *From left to right:* boating in Georgia; public gardens in Augusta; a black bear; Forsythe Park, Savannah; a rural landscape; George Smith State Park.

and is home to wild animals such as black bears and alligators, to name only the largest. Apart from the swamps and some of the higher hills, the coastal plain is mostly farmland. Its climate is warm with high humidity.

The Piedmont Plateau

The Piedmont occupies about 30 percent of Georgia. It lies between the coastal plains and the more mountainous regions farther north. It is a land of rolling hills, some quite large. The most distinctive is Stone Mountain, near Atlanta. Its mass of exposed granite rises 1,683 feet (512 m) above sea level. Flatter areas in the Piedmont are mostly farms, while the higher hills are covered with pine forests. Generally, the temperatures are cooler at the higher altitudes.

The Blue Ridge Province

The Blue Ridge Province includes the Blue Ridge Mountains and the adjoining valley. It occupies only about 5 percent of Georgia but is considered one of the most beautiful parts of the state and the country. The state's highest mountain — Brasstown Bald Mountain at 4,784 feet (1,458 m) — is there. It also has the state's highest falls, Amicalola Falls, which drop 729 feet (222 m). Few people live in the Blue Ridge Province, but many come to visit its natural splendors.

The Ridge and Valley Province

The Ridge and Valley Province of the northwest is distinguished by a series of high ridges and lowland valleys. The rocks that make up the ridges are highly resistant to erosion, while the lowlands are made up of softer rocks that erode more quickly. The main valley is the Rome Valley. Ridges include Taylor Ridge and Pigeon Mountain. Most of the ridges are covered with forests. The valleys where soil is rich are dotted with many farms.

Average January temperature
Atlanta: 41°F (5°C)
Savannah: 49°F (9.4°C)

Average July temperature
Atlanta: 79°F (26°C)
Savannah: 82°F (28°C)

Average yearly rainfall
Atlanta:
  48 inches (121 cm)
Savannah
  51 inches (129 cm)

Average yearly snowfall
Atlanta:
  1.5 inches (3.8 cm)
Savannah:
  0.3 inches (0.76 cm)

DID YOU KNOW?

Georgia's Blue Ridge Mountains are now only about a quarter of their former height, thanks to one hundred million years of erosion.

Largest Lakes

J. Strom Thurmond Lake
70,000 acres
  (28,327 ha)

Hartwell Lake
56,000 acres
  (22,661 ha)

West Point Lake
26,000 acres (10,521 ha)

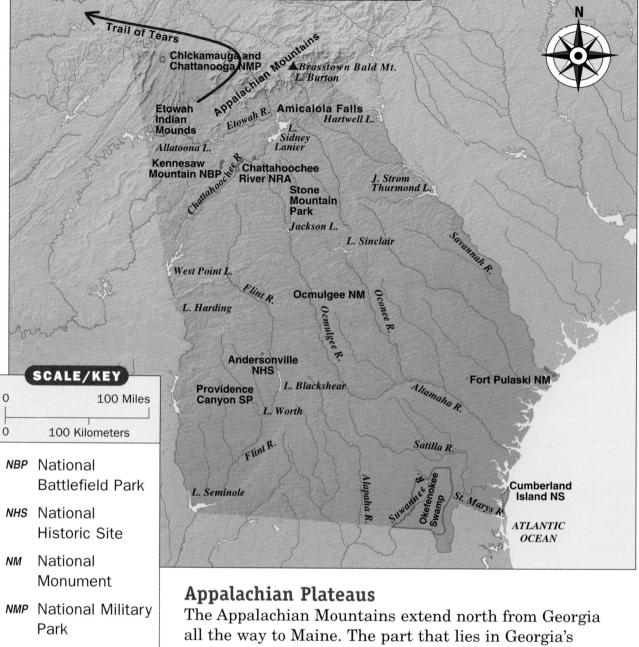

Trail of Tears

Chickamauga and
Chattanooga NMP

Appalachian Mountains

▲ Brasstown Bald Mt.
L. Burton

Etowah
Indian
Mounds

Etowah R.

Amicalola Falls
Hartwell L.

L.
Sidney
Lanier

Allatoona L.

Kennesaw
Mountain NBP

Chattahoochee R.

Chattahoochee
River NRA

J. Strom
Thurmond L.

Stone
Mountain
Park

Jackson L.

L. Sinclair

Savannah R.

West Point L.

Flint R.

Ocmulgee NM

Oconee R.

L. Harding

Ocmulgee R.

Andersonville
NHS

Providence
Canyon SP

L. Blackshear

L. Worth

Altamaha R.

Fort Pulaski NM

Flint R.

Satilla R.

L. Seminole

Alapaha R.

Suwannee R.

Okefenokee
Swamp

St. Marys R.

Cumberland
Island NS

ATLANTIC
OCEAN

N

SCALE/KEY

| 0 | 100 Miles |
| 0 | 100 Kilometers |

NBP	National Battlefield Park
NHS	National Historic Site
NM	National Monument
NMP	National Military Park
NRA	National Recreation Area
NS	National Seashore
SP	State Park
▲	Highest Point
	Mountains

Appalachian Plateaus

The Appalachian Mountains extend north from Georgia
all the way to Maine. The part that lies in Georgia's
extreme northwest is known as the Cumberland Plateau.
Once isolated mountain country, the area is becoming
increasingly developed. Cooler temperatures make the
mountains a refuge from the sometimes sweltering
conditions down south.

Plants and Animals

Almost all of Georgia was forested before European
settlement. Today, about 66 percent still is. Early in the
twentieth century, cotton was grown in such huge quantities

that the soil in many fields became seriously depleted. Since then, many cotton fields have been planted with other crops in rotation, others have become pasture for grazing animals, or even reverted to forest. A major reforestation effort was made throughout the state. Trees help slow erosion and protect wildlife. They can also be good business — Georgia's lumber and paper industry has benefited, too.

The diversity of Georgia's terrain makes the state home to many different kinds of plants. Marsh grasses grow along the Atlantic coast, while red gum, tupelo, and cypress trees thrive in the swamplands. Georgia is famous for its pine trees, which grow in large forests in the western part of the state.

The diversity of Georgia's plant life is matched by its wildlife. Sea turtles inhabit the shoreline, while bears have been seen on golf courses in the suburbs as well as in the woods. The swamps of the south are home to alligators as well as waterbirds such as herons and egrets. Small mammals, such as raccoons and rabbits, can be found throughout the state. Georgia's waterways provide habitats for many types of freshwater fish found in the United States, including snook and bonefish.

Major Rivers

Chattahoochee River
436 miles (701 km)

Savannah River
314 miles (505 km)

Suwannee River
250 miles (400 km)

▼ Providence Canyon State Park in Lumpkin is sometimes called the "Little Grand Canyon." It looks similar to the Grand Canyon but is much smaller.

Cotton and CNN

> The commanding position of the State of Georgia in the matter of internal communication of the Union is now apparent to every one.
>
> — De Bow's Review, *a weekly business magazine, 1849*

Georgia's economy has been transformed several times in its history. It was overwhelmingly an agricultural state until well into the twentieth century. Early European settlers grew indigo, rice, and sugarcane. It was cotton, however, that became "king" of Georgia's economy during the nineteenth century. The king was overthrown in the 1920s when boll weevil infestations destroyed the cotton crop. Crop yields had also been on the decline because years of intensive cotton cultivation had made the soil less fertile.

Georgia's oldest major industry is textiles, a natural outgrowth of its cotton cultivation. Textile manufacturing began in the 1830s and became increasingly important later in the century. Today, carpets are a major product — more than half the nation's tufted carpet is produced in Georgia. World War II stimulated the growth of other industries in the state, including the military and transportation industries. Service industries are becoming ever more important, especially in the Atlanta area.

Agriculture, Forestry, and Mining

There are many farms in Georgia — about fifty thousand — but most are very small. In 2000, only 35 percent had yearly sales of $10,000 or more. Poultry, livestock, and livestock products generate about 60 percent of the yearly farm income, with crops accounting for the rest. The state's most valuable farm product is poultry. Georgia specializes in young "eating" chickens called broilers, and Georgia is among the top three producers of broiler chickens in the United States. Georgia is also a leader in nut production,

Top Employers (of workers age sixteen and over)	
Services	29.5%
Wholesale and retail trade	21.5%
Manufacturing	18.9%
Transportation, communications, and other public utilities	8.6%
Construction	6.9%
Finance, insurance, and real estate	6.5%
Public Administration	5.4%
Agriculture, forestry, and fisheries	2.4%
Mining	0.3%

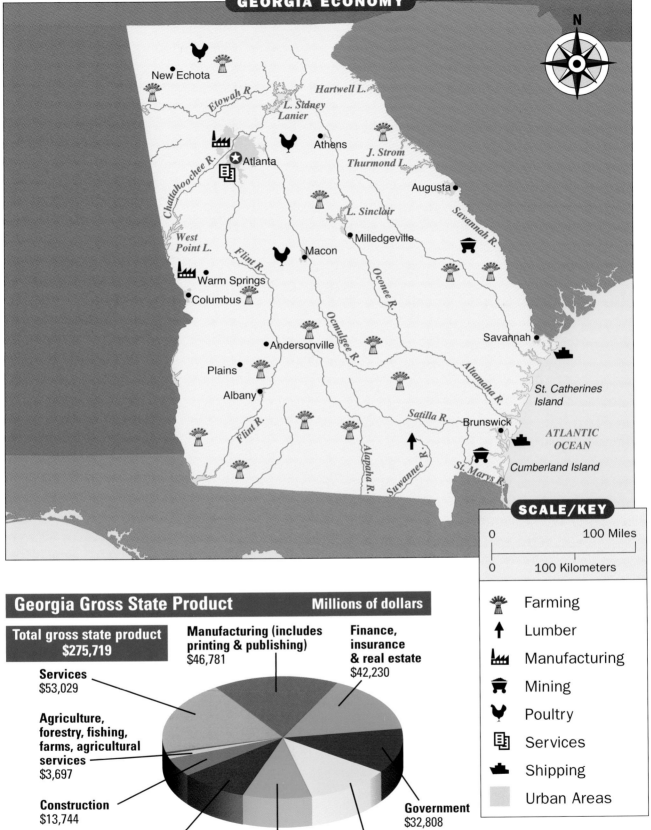

GEORGIA ECONOMY

New Echota

Etowah R.

Hartwell L.

L. Sidney Lanier

Atlanta

Athens

J. Strom Thurmond L.

Augusta

Chattahoochee R.

L. Sinclair

Milledgeville

Savannah R.

West Point L.

Flint R.

Macon

Oconee R.

Warm Springs

Columbus

Ocmulgee R.

Andersonville

Plains

Albany

Flint R.

Alapaha R.

Satilla R.

Suwannee R.

St. Marys R.

Savannah

St. Catherines Island

Brunswick

ATLANTIC OCEAN

Cumberland Island

Altamaha R.

N

SCALE/KEY

0   100 Miles

0   100 Kilometers

- Farming
- Lumber
- Manufacturing
- Mining
- Poultry
- Services
- Shipping
- Urban Areas

Georgia Gross State Product   Millions of dollars

Total gross state product $275,719

Services $53,029

Agriculture, forestry, fishing, farms, agricultural services $3,697

Construction $13,744

Mining $1,244

Wholesale trade $24,967

Retail trade $25,743

Manufacturing (includes printing & publishing) $46,781

Finance, insurance & real estate $42,230

Government $32,808

Transportation & utilities $31,476

particularly peanuts and pecans. Peanuts are the state's most valuable crop. Since methods were found to control boll weevils, cotton has reemerged to become Georgia's second most valuable crop. Georgia is also famous for its peaches; in fact, one of its nicknames is the "Peach State." Peach County, near Macon, is the hub of Georgia's peach orchards.

Manufacturing

Processed foods and beverages — such as baked goods, beer, soft drinks, frozen chickens, and peanut butter — are Georgia's leading manufactured products. Ranking second among the state's manufactured products are textiles. Georgia is second only to North Carolina in textile production. The third most valuable of Georgia's manufactured products is transportation equipment. That includes motor vehicles such as cars, and also machinery used in advanced airplanes and spacecraft.

Paper mills play an important part in the economy. Cellophane and rayon are important by-products of paper production. Lumber mills produce building lumber and hardwood flooring. Other goods made in Georgia include industrial machinery, electronic equipment, chemicals, metal products, and bricks and tiles. Overall there are nearly ten thousand manufacturing plants in Georgia.

Timber is cut each year from Georgia's commercial woodlands, which have expanded in recent years due to a well-managed renewal program. Most of the timber is softwood that is pulped to make paper. Mining makes up less than one percent of Georgia's gross state product, but several important commodities are produced. Clay and stone are the most valuable. The state leads the United States in clay production, specifically in kaolin, a clay used to add a sheen to porcelain and paper products. High-quality granite and marble are quarried in northern Georgia. Other mineral products include barite, feldspar, and mica.

▲ Workers in a Georgia cotton field circa 1917.

Things Were Rotten in the Land of Cotton Till . . .

In 1793, Eli Whitney visited the plantation of Catharine Greene, widow of General Nathanael Greene, near Savannah. There Whitney built a machine that changed Georgia and the world, helping to start the Industrial Revolution. The cotton gin separated the seeds from the fibers of the short-staple cotton plant, work that until then was done by hand. With the gin, cotton could be cleaned so efficiently that it became the basis of the region's economy. Whitney, however, made little profit from his invention, which was copied by many others. According to Whitney, "An invention can be so valuable as to be worthless to the inventor." Some scholars are convinced that one of the crucial parts of the design was Catharine Greene's idea.

Transportation, Services, and Tourism

Railroad, highway, and air transportation routes in the southeastern United States all converge on Atlanta. The city, in fact, began its existence as little more than a railroad hub. In 1827, surveyors for the Western and Atlantic Railroad chose the spot that would become Atlanta as one of the endpoints for their new line. By 1860, Atlanta's Union Depot was the major hub for the southeast, and five railroad lines converged in the city. Atlanta is now also the site of William B. Hartsfield International Airport, one of the busiest airports in the world. Georgia's main seaports are Savannah and Brunswick. The state also has about 113,000 miles (181,817 km) of federal, state, and local roads.

Service industries now account for the largest share of Georgia's economy as measured by gross state product. That share is equally divided among community, business, and personal services. Georgia's service industries are heavily concentrated in the Atlanta metropolitan area, which has lately had one of the highest economic growth rates in the nation. Atlanta is a fast-growing center of finance, trade, and transportation. Companies with headquarters in Atlanta include Coca-Cola, Georgia-Pacific, United Parcel Service, Home Depot, Delta Air Lines, and Cable News Network (CNN).

Tourism is not just about enjoyment. It is also a major economic activity. About forty-three million visitors come to Georgia every year and spend about sixteen billion dollars. The 1996 Summer Olympic Games, especially, drew the world's attention to Atlanta and Georgia. Tourists are drawn mostly to the coast, the city of Atlanta, and the Blue Ridge Mountains.

▲ A textile mill along Augusta's canal. Augusta was one of the first southern cities to begin manufacturing one of the South's most important crops — cotton — into textiles rather than shipping the cotton to manufacturing centers in the northeast and around the world.

Made in Georgia

Leading farm products and crops
Poultry
Peanuts
Pecans
Cotton
Peaches
Watermelons

Other products
Processed foods
Textiles
Transportation equipment

Major Airports		
Airport	Location	Passengers per year (2000)
Hartsfield Atlanta International	Atlanta	80,162,407
Savannah International	Savannah	1,774,190

A Dynamic State

Resolved, That we were born free, have all the feelings of men, and are entitled to all the natural rights of mankind.

— *Provincial Congress Resolutions, July 4, 1775*

Georgia has had ten state constitutions, adopted in 1777, 1789, 1798, 1861, 1865, 1868, 1877, 1945, 1976, and 1982. Nearly half of those adoptions were made during the turbulent Civil War and Reconstruction period. In 1983, Georgians made an important change to their constitution. Before this time, changes in local laws had to be made through amendments to the state constitution. This meant that a great many amendments were passed that affected only small numbers of people. In 1983, Georgians adopted a constitutional amendment that disallowed further local amendments. All constitutional amendments require a two-thirds majority vote in each house of the legislature, and also approval by a majority of voters in a general election.

The system of government in Georgia — just like that of the U.S. federal government — is divided into three branches: executive, legislative, and judicial. The executive branch administers laws, the legislative branch makes laws, and the judicial branch interprets laws.

The Executive Branch

The governor of Georgia is the state's chief executive. The governor is the director of the budget, deciding how state money is collected and distributed. Another executive power is the right to veto proposed legislation. The legislature can override the governor's veto by a two-thirds majority vote in both houses. The governor also has extensive powers to appoint members of boards and commissions, although usually the state senate has to approve the choices. In addition, there are seven other elected officials plus a five-member public service commission in the executive branch. This commission is one of the state's eight executive boards,

The Constitution

"To perpetuate the principles of free government, insure justice to all, preserve peace, promote the interest and happiness of the citizen and of the family, and transmit to posterity the enjoyment of liberty, we the people of Georgia, relying upon the protection and guidance of Almighty God, do ordain and establish this Constitution."

— *Preamble to the 1982 Georgia State Constitution*

Elected Posts in the Executive Branch		
Office	Length of Term	Term Limits
Governor	4 years	2 consecutive terms
Lieutenant Governor	4 years	2 consecutive terms
Secretary of State	4 years	none
Commissioner of Insurance	4 years	none
Attorney General	4 years	none
Superintendent of Schools	4 years	none
Commissioner of Labor	4 years	none
Commissioner of Agriculture	4 years	none
Public Service Commissioner	6 years	none

and members are elected to six-year terms. The public service commission regulates companies that provide key public services, such as transportation, electricity, and telephone service.

The Legislative Branch

The Georgia state legislature is called the General Assembly. It is composed of a Senate with fifty-six members and a House of Representatives with one hundred eighty members. The General Assembly meets annually in Atlanta, beginning every year on the second Monday in January and continuing no longer than forty days. That is the regular session, but special sessions can also be called by the governor or a three-fifths vote of the legislature.

The legislature is responsible for proposing and passing new laws, as well as approving the state budget and allocating funds to carry it out.

The Judicial Branch

The judicial branch consists of judges presiding over courts, with each court subject to review by a higher court. The state supreme court is the highest court in Georgia. It makes the final decision in all cases except those where state law conflicts with federal law. The seven supreme court justices are elected

▼ Construction on Georgia's state capitol began in 1884, and the building was formally dedicated in 1889. In 1977 it was designated a National Historic Landmark.

to six-year terms. The justices then elect one among them to be chief justice. The other six justices are known as associate justices.

The court of appeals is the state's second highest court. The twelve judges of the court of appeals are also elected to six-year terms. Below the court of appeals are forty-eight superior courts that function as the state's chief trial courts. Each of these courts has from two to nineteen judges, depending on the district. Superior court judges are elected to four-year terms.

Other courts include county probate courts, city courts, and juvenile courts. The governor, with the Senate's approval, appoints some judges on these lower courts.

Local Government

Government is also divided in another way: federal, state, and local. While the federal government of the United States has powers over the whole nation, state governments such as Georgia's have powers over their own state matters. Within the states, too, there are local governments with powers over special local matters. All in all, there are more than twelve hundred governments in Georgia, from the state government down to the municipalities.

Counties are one form of local government in the United States. Georgia has 159 counties. That number is second only to Texas, which has 254. Counties, the largest general-purpose form of local government, perform some state functions such as issuing marriage certificates, conducting elections, and providing county residents with various other local services. Some counties are even quite similar to cities in the types of services they provide. Boards of commissioners govern 156 of Georgia's 159 counties.

Georgia also has about 531 cities, towns, and villages, generally called municipalities. Their charters (rules) used to be written by the state legislature. The legislature passed a law in 1965, however, that gave municipalities the power to determine their own charters. Of course, local charters

General Assembly			
House	**Number of Members**	**Length of Term**	**Term Limits**
Senate	56 senators	2 years	No limit
House of Representatives	180 representatives	2 years	No limit

The White House via Georgia

JIMMY CARTER (1977–1981)

James Earl Carter was born in Plains in 1924. He attended the U.S. Naval Academy. During his naval career, he rose to the rank of lieutenant. Returning to Plains in 1953, Carter ran the family peanut farm. He was elected to the Georgia senate in 1962 and became Georgia's governor in 1971. Running as a Democrat, he was elected the thirty-ninth U.S. president on November 2, 1976. Carter's legacy includes helping to negotiate a peace treaty between Egypt and Israel and establishing major educational and environmental programs. Problems included the Iran hostage crisis, inflation, and an energy crisis. After losing his bid for re-election, he established the Carter Center, which promotes peace and human rights. He is also known for his work with Habitat for Humanity, a group that builds houses for the poor.

cannot conflict with state laws. The most common form of municipal government in Georgia is a five-member board.

National Representation

Like all states, Georgia has two senators in the U.S. Senate. As of the 2002 elections, the state will have thirteen representatives in the U.S. House of Representatives, an increase of two. As of the 2004 presidential election, the state will have fifteen Electoral College votes, up from thirteen. The number of representatives and electoral college votes is increasing as a result of the fast-growing population.

Georgia Politics

As Georgia's wealth has increased, there has been a major political shift. Since Reconstruction, the Democratic party has dominated Georgia politics, but that is changing, as it is through much of the South. African-American voters, however, still vote heavily for Democrats. In 2002, Atlantans made history by electing Democrat Shirley Franklin mayor. Franklin became the city's first female mayor and the first African-American woman mayor of a major city in the southeast.

▼ From 1864 to 1865, Macon served as Georgia's capital city. The buildings below housed this temporary government.

The New South

> For the entire state of Georgia, having the premiere of *Gone With the Wind* on home ground was like winning the Battle of Atlanta seventy-five years late.
>
> — *Anne Edwards, biographer of Margaret Mitchell, in* Road to Tara, *1983*

What will you find in Georgia today? A lot depends on the trail you take. One place to start is the Chieftains Trail in northwest Georgia. It highlights the history of the Native Americans who once inhabited the area. It became an official state historical trail in 1988. That was 150 years after the Cherokee were forced away to Oklahoma on the "Trail of Tears." The Etowah Indian Mounds are temple mounds that were the ceremonial center of the local Mississippian culture. Also on the trail is the town of New Echota, which became the capital of the Cherokee Nation in 1825. There you can find the reconstructed Supreme Courthouse, the Council House, and the print shop where the *Cherokee Phoenix* was printed.

The Antebellum Trail winds through Athens, Madison, Milledgeville, and Macon. Antebellum means "pre-war," in this case the time before the Civil War. The antebellum era was described in the famous book and movie *Gone with the Wind*. Georgia's first state capitol building, grand mansions, and magnolia-shaded gardens line the trail. The Morgan County African-American Museum and many old slave quarters reveal another side of the Old South.

▼ Visitors explore the burial mound at the Ocmulgee National Monument in Macon.

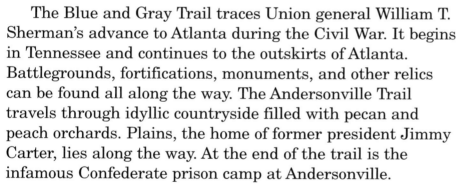

The Blue and Gray Trail traces Union general William T. Sherman's advance to Atlanta during the Civil War. It begins in Tennessee and continues to the outskirts of Atlanta. Battlegrounds, fortifications, monuments, and other relics can be found all along the way. The Andersonville Trail travels through idyllic countryside filled with pecan and peach orchards. Plains, the home of former president Jimmy Carter, lies along the way. At the end of the trail is the infamous Confederate prison camp at Andersonville.

Off the coast of Georgia are the Sea Islands, which have a rich cultural heritage and great natural beauty. The Sea Islands are now a combination of private resorts and national parks. In the nineteenth century, these islands were the center of the Gullah culture, created by former slaves. Gullah is a dialect that blends elements of seventeenth and eighteenth century English with African languages such as Igbo and Yoruba. The words *voodoo*, *gumbo* (a type of stew), and *goober* (a word for peanut) are all words from the Gullah dialect.

Seabrook Historical Village, on the Georgia coast, is a living museum that celebrates African-American life in Georgia after the Civil War. Visitors to this 104 acre (42 ha) site will get a unique glimpse into how former slaves established new lives in freedom.

The New South

This Greek Revival house was the Athens home of Henry W. Grady (1850–1889). He was the editor of the *Atlanta Constitution* and the leading proponent of the "New South." The New South was the term for a vision of Southern culture in which the injustice and economic stagnation of the pre-Civil War slavery era were replaced by a racially integrated and industrialized society. In 1886, Grady expressed this vision in a speech in which he announced that "There was the South of slavery and secession — that South is dead. There is now a South of union and freedom — that South, thank God, is living, breathing, and growing every hour."

The Elachee Nature Center in Gainesville offers 1,200 acres (485 ha) of woodlands where visitors may participate in educational programs to learn all about the the state's complex ecosystems.

▲ Atlanta's High Museum of Art.

Libraries and Museums

The early colony's leaders established Georgia's first library in 1736. An extensive network of libraries has since developed. The largest is the Atlanta-Fulton Public Library, which was established by the Young Men's Library Association in 1867 and opened to the general public in 1902. Other libraries include the state archives in Atlanta, the Hargrett Rare Book and Manuscript Library of the University of Georgia, and the Georgia Historical Society Library in Savannah.

Founded in 1905, the High Museum of Art in Atlanta is among the largest art galleries in the country. Its permanent collection includes European Old Masters, but the museum is best known for its collections of nineteenth- and twentieth-century Americana — decorative and folk art. Distinguished collections of American paintings can

DID YOU KNOW?

In Athens, Georgia, there is a white oak tree that "owns itself." In the late 1800s Colonel W. H. Jackson made an unusual stipulation in his will. "For and in consideration of the great love I bear this tree," he wrote, "and the great desire I have for its protection for all time, I convey entire possession of itself and the land within eight feet of it on all sides."

also be found in the Georgia Museum of Art at the University of Georgia, the state's official museum, and at the Telfair Museum of Art in Savannah. The Atlanta History Center owns two historic homes and two historic playhouses that give visitors a sense of what life was like for Atlantans of all ages in the nineteenth and twentieth centuries. SciTrek in Atlanta is a science and technology museum that offers more than one hundred twenty interactive exhibits. Visitors can freeze their own shadows and create lightning in a jar.

Communications

About 250 newspapers are published in Georgia. Most are published only once a week, but about thirty-six are published every day. James Johnston, the early colony's official printer, published Georgia's first newspaper in Savannah in 1763. It was called the *Georgia Gazette.* The oldest newspaper that has continued to be published is the *Augusta Chronicle,* which began in 1785 as the *Augusta Gazette.* In 2001, two of the most popular newspapers in Georgia, the *Atlanta Journal* and the *Atlanta Constitution,* merged to become one newspaper. Easily Georgia's most prominent media organization, however, is the Cable News

▼ The *Challenger* Learning Center is part of the Coca-Cola Space Science Center in Columbus. Visitors can take "trips" to the Moon, rendezvous with a comet, and explore Earth as if from space.

▶ Born in Dawson, Otis Redding moved to Macon at the age of five, first singing at the Vineville Baptist Church and eventually becoming an international rhythm-and-blues sensation.

Network (CNN), which broadcasts from Atlanta to audiences all around the world.

Music and Theater

The Atlanta Symphony Orchestra is widely considered to be the leading orchestra in the southeast. Many of the state's other cities and universities also support symphony orchestras. Both Atlanta and Augusta have opera companies. While the Atlanta Ballet has gone through several names since it was formed in 1929, it is nevertheless the oldest continuously operating dance company in the nation.

Midtown Atlanta has many live-performance venues hosting local, national, and international acts. Popular musicians from Georgia include Otis Redding, Gladys Knight, and Little Richard. Athens is known as a creative center for contemporary music. The renowned alternative rock groups R.E.M. and the B-52s both developed there.

In Macon, the Georgia Music Hall of Fame celebrates the state's musical heritage from Native American music to the present. Among the rare instruments included in the museum's large collection are an eight-foot guitar, a red sequined suit once worn by James Brown, and former U.S. president Bill Clinton's saxophone.

Sports

Georgia is a great sporting state, with many professional sports teams. Atlanta's most brilliant sporting moment

Sport	Team	Home
Baseball	Atlanta Braves	Turner Field, Atlanta
Basketball	Atlanta Hawks	Philips Arena, Atlanta
Football	Atlanta Falcons	Georgia Dome, Atlanta
Hockey	Atlanta Thrashers	Philips Arena, Atlanta

came when it played host to the 1996 Summer Olympic Games. Every year, Atlanta hosts the Peach Bowl college football game. Augusta is the site of the annual Masters Golf Tournament, which draws fans from all around the world. River Race Augusta is a world-class boating event held on the Savannah River.

The Braves began playing major league baseball in Atlanta in 1966. Before that, they had been the Boston Braves and the Milwaukee Braves. It was as a Brave that Hank Aaron hit his 715th home run in 1974, passing Babe Ruth's record for most career home runs. The Braves won the World Series in 1995.

The Atlanta Falcons, the state's National Football League (NFL) team, began playing in 1966. The team name was selected through a statewide contest that was won by a schoolteacher, Julia Elliot, from Griffin. She recommended that the team be named after the falcon, because this bird "never drops its prey." The Falcons appeared in the 1999 Super Bowl.

The Atlanta Hawks of the National Basketball Association (NBA) arrived in town from St. Louis in 1968. In 1982, the team acquired Dominique Wilkins, who would be their star player for the next ten years. Wilkins is the highest scorer in the team's history. The Hawks are owned by Atlanta billionaire Ted Turner, who also owns the Braves. Atlanta's newest team is the Thrashers of the National Hockey League (NHL), who began play in the 1999–2000 season.

COBB, DETROIT

Georgia Greats

Ty Cobb, nicknamed "The Georgia Peach," may be the best baseball player of all time. His accomplishments are amazing. He won twelve batting titles and hit over .300 in twenty-three straight seasons. He also had three .400 seasons, topped by a .420 season in 1911. His lifetime average was .366. During his twenty-four year career, he stole 892 bases. Cobb played primarily for the Detroit Tigers.

"**H**ammerin' Hank" Aaron of the Milwaukee, then the Atlanta, Braves, as well as the Milwaukee Brewers, earned his nickname by hitting 755 home runs during his twenty-three-year baseball career. He also established twelve other major league career records, including most games, at-bats, total bases, and RBIs. He earned National League MVP honors in 1957 and appeared in a record twenty-four All-Star Games.

▶ Hank Aaron hitting his 715th home run in 1974 to break Babe Ruth's career record of 714.

Great Georgians

Oh! thy waters, thy sweet valley waters
Are dearer than any to me;
For thy daughters, thy sweet-smiling daughters,
Oh! Georgia! give beauty to thee.
— *Thomas Holly Chivers, Writer, 1845*

Following are only a few of the thousands of people who were born, died, or spent much of their lives in Georgia and made extraordinary contributions to the state and the nation.

JOHN WESLEY
EVANGELIST

BORN: *June 17, 1703, Epworth, England*
DIED: *March 2, 1791, London, England*

John Wesley was an influential Christian leader. He came with his brother from England to Savannah in the new colony of Georgia, in 1735. He was greatly influenced by the religion of the Moravians, who had found refuge there. With his brother, Charles, Wesley founded the Methodist movement. It declares that each person is accepted as a child of God. Wesley's influence continues today with a large number of Methodist churches in Georgia. The Methodist organization also extends around the world.

REBECCA ANN FELTON
SENATOR

BORN: *June 10, 1835, near Decatur*
DIED: *January 24, 1930, Atlanta*

A graduate of Madison Female College in Georgia, Rebecca Ann Latimer married a physician and Methodist minister named Dr. William Felton. The couple had five children, but only one survived to adulthood. After the Civil War, Dr. Felton won a seat in the U.S. Congress with the help of his wife, who was also his campaign manager and speechwriter.

Mrs. Felton eventually became as powerful a figure as her husband. She was outspoken on many issues, including women's right to vote and campaign reforms. When one of Georgia's U.S. senators died in office, the governor of Georgia ceremonially appointed Mrs. Felton to the vacant post. At age eighty-seven, she thus became the first female U.S. senator, on November 21, 1922. She held the position for one day, until the newly elected senator could take office.

Doc Holliday
GAMBLER AND GUNFIGHTER
BORN: *August 14, 1851, Griffin*
DIED: *November 8, 1887, Glenwood Springs, CO*

John Henry Holliday was born into a wealthy family. After finishing his education as a dentist, he found that he had contracted a severe case of tuberculosis. Dry climates were believed to slow the often-deadly disease's progress, so Holliday moved out West. Believing he had little to lose, he made a living as a gambler. This led to many violent conflicts, which he always lived to tell about. The most famous of his exploits was the gunfight at the O.K. Corral, where he and the Earp brothers, including Wyatt Earp, defeated the Clanton gang. After Holliday's death (amazingly, from natural causes), a stream of books and movies made him into a legend of the Wild West.

Juliette Gordon Low
GIRL SCOUTS FOUNDER
BORN: *October 31, 1860, Savannah*
DIED: *January 17, 1927, Savannah*

From an early age, Juliette Gordon wrote poems and plays, acted, and sketched. In 1886, she married William Low. She met Sir Robert Baden-Powell, founder of the Boy Scouts and Girl Guides in England, in 1911. On March 12, 1912, she organized the first U.S. Girl Guide troop in Savannah. The name was changed to Girl Scouts the following year. The Girl Scout movement brought girls outdoors, where they learned about nature and their own abilities. Low was ahead of her time in training Girl Scouts not only for traditional homemaking roles but also for professional careers in the arts, sciences, and business. From eighteen girls in 1912, the Girl Scouts have grown to more than three million members.

Oliver Hardy
ACTOR AND COMEDIAN
BORN: *January 18, 1892, Harlem*
DIED: *August 7, 1957, North Hollywood, CA*

When Norvell "Babe" Hardy was eight years old, he ran away from home and toured with a singing group called Coburn's Minstrels. Later, he was employed at the Electric Theater in Milledgeville, as a projectionist and singer. Deciding to become a part of the images he saw on the screen, he made his way to Hollywood and changed his name to Oliver Hardy. Standing more than 6 feet (1.8 meters) tall and weighing up to 300 pounds (136 kilograms), he was teamed with Stan Laurel, a much thinner man, in 1926. Laurel and Hardy then became a great comic duo. In 1928, they released eleven films, and even more in 1929. Their worldwide popularity continued to grow in the 1930s. *The Music Box* won the Academy Award for Best Live Action Comedy Short Subject in 1932.

MARGARET MITCHELL
AUTHOR

BORN: *November 8, 1900, Atlanta*
DIED: *August 16, 1949, Atlanta*

Margaret Mitchell began her writing career as a journalist in 1922 for the *Atlanta Journal* under the name Peggy Mitchell. From 1926 to 1929, she wrote *Gone with the Wind,* but it was not published until 1936. The novel then broke sales records and was awarded the 1937 Pulitzer Prize. It tells the story of the Civil War and Reconstruction from the Southern point of view. In 1939, the novel was adapted into a popular film that won nine major and two special Oscars. Although *Gone With the Wind* brought fame and fortune, Mitchell and her husband lived quietly and rarely traveled.

FLANNERY O'CONNOR
WRITER

BORN: *March 25, 1925, Savannah*
DIED: *August 3, 1964, Milledgeville*

Mary Flannery O'Connor spent most of her life in Milledgeville, raising peacocks and writing. Her novels and volumes of short stories place her among the great U.S. writers of the twentieth century. Her novels are *Wise Blood* (1952) and *The Violent Bear It Away* (1960). The short-story collections are *A Good Man Is Hard to Find* (1955) and *Everything That Rises Must Converge* (1965). Her works are usually set in the rural South and often deal with religious themes. During her later years, she wrote under the constant threat of death from a disabling case of lupus. Her reputation as a writer has continued to grow since her death.

JASPER JOHNS
ARTIST

BORN: *May 15, 1930, Augusta*

Jasper Johns was twenty-four when he moved to New York to pursue a career as an artist. His 1954–55 painting *Flag* was the first in a series of paintings of the U.S. flag that shook up the art world. Targets, numbers, and letters were also common early subjects. His art was considered a break from Abstract Expressionism, which was a dominant style of art at the time. He has been hailed as the father of the New York School. Johns's paintings, prints, drawings, and sculptures are among the most influential in late-twentieth-century art.

RAY CHARLES
MUSICIAN

BORN: *September 23, 1930, Albany*

Ray Charles lost his sight before his seventh birthday. He attended Saint Augustine's school for the deaf and blind in Florida, where he learned to read Braille and compose music. He then set out on the road as a musician. By the early 1960s, he had become a star.

His first hit was "Georgia on My Mind" in 1960. Although usually associated with blues and rhythm and blues, Ray Charles's sound crosses over into gospel, jazz, rock, and even country and western. He has toured the world and has won multiple Grammy awards.

JULIAN BOND
CIVIL RIGHTS ACTIVIST
BORN: *January 14, 1940, Nashville, TN*

Julian Bond is the son of educator Dr. Horace Bond, the first African-American president of the oldest African-American college in the United States, Lincoln University in Pennsylvania. Julian Bond graduated from Morehouse College in Atlanta. While a student in 1960, Bond helped to found the Committee on Appeal for Human Rights (COAHR). Bond and COAHR staged nonviolent protests against racial segregation in Atlanta and won the integration of public parks, movie theaters, and restaurants. Bond then helped found the Student Nonviolent Coordinating Committee (SNCC), which was one of the most influential organizations in the 1960s Civil Rights Movement. Bond was elected to the Georgia House of Representatives in 1965, but his fellow legislators would not allow him to take office because he was against U.S. involvement in the Vietnam War. In 1966, the U.S. Supreme Court ruled that Bond must be allowed to serve. In 1974, Bond was elected to the Georgia Senate and served until 1987. When he left the Senate, he had held office longer than any other African American in U.S. history. Bond continues to write and speak out for the expansion of civil rights.

NEWT GINGRICH
POLITICAL LEADER
BORN: *June 17, 1943, Harrisburg, PA*

Newton Leroy Gingrich was elected to the U.S. House of Representatives in 1978 from Marietta, Georgia. Gingrich designed the Republicans' 1994 "Contract with America" political program, which helped the party gain control of both the House and the Senate for the first time since 1954. Gingrich became Speaker of the House on January 4, 1995, the first Republican to hold the post in more than forty years. In 1997, Gingrich faced ethics charges and became the first sitting Speaker ever to be disciplined by the House. Gingrich served in the House until 1999.

JESSYE NORMAN
SINGER
BORN: *September 15, 1945, Augusta*

Jessye Norman is one of the world's most admired singers. She began singing as a member of her church choir when she was four. In 1967, she graduated with honors from Howard University in Atlanta and then went on to the prestigious Peabody Conservatory of Music. Her operatic debut was in Berlin, Germany, in 1969. Although best known for her opera performances, Norman is also acclaimed for recitals of African-American spiritual music. In 1997, she was the youngest person to win honors from the Kennedy Center in Washington. Norman is famous for the suppleness and range of her soprano voice and resists categorization. "Pigeonholing," she once said, "is only interesting to pigeons."

Georgia
History At-A-Glance

1540
A Spanish expedition under Hernando de Soto crosses through Georgia.

1776
Georgians Lyman Hall, Button Gwinnett, and George Walton sign the Declaration of Independence.

1793
Eli Whitney invents the cotton gin.

1828
The nation's first gold rush begins in northeastern Georgia.

1861
Georgia secedes from the Union.

1868
Atlanta becomes the permanent capital of Georgia.

1733
Oglethorpe establishes Georgia colony at Savannah.

1785
University of Georgia is chartered.

1821
Sequoya invents a Cherokee alphabet.

1838–39
Cherokee are expelled from Georgia on the "Trail of Tears."

1864
Sherman captures Atlanta and marches through the state to Savannah.

1881
Atlanta holds the "World's Fair and Great International Cotton Exposition."

1600 **1700** **1800**

1492
Christopher Columbus comes to New World.

1607
Capt. John Smith and three ships land on Virginia coast and start first English settlement in New World — Jamestown.

1754–63
French and Indian War.

1776
Declaration of Independence adopted July 4.

1787
U.S. Constitution written.

1773
Boston Tea Party.

1777
Articles of Confederation adopted by Continental Congress.

1812–14
War of 1812.

United States
History At-A-Glance

1913
The boll weevil arrives in Georgia and begins to destroy the cotton crop.

1925
Atlanta converts Candler Field racetrack into an airport.

1939
The movie *Gone With the Wind* premieres in Atlanta.

1966
The Falcons, an NFL expansion team, begin play in Atlanta.

1972
Andrew Young becomes Georgia's first African-American congressman since Reconstruction.

1983
Georgians amend their constitution and no longer allow local amendments.

1919
The Candler family sells the Coca-Cola company for $25 million.

1929
Delta Air Lines begins passenger service between Atlanta and Dallas.

1964
Dr. Martin Luther King, Jr., is awarded the Nobel Peace Prize.

1969
First delivery of a Lockheed-Georgia C-5A is made to the U.S. Air Force.

1976
Georgia native Jimmy Carter is elected president of the United States.

1996
Atlanta hosts Summer Olympic Games.

1800   **1900**   **2000**

1848
Gold discovered in California draws eighty thousand prospectors in the 1849 Gold Rush.

1869
Transcontinental railroad completed.

1929
Stock market crash ushers in Great Depression.

1950–53
U.S. fights in the Korean War.

2000
George W. Bush wins the closest presidential election in history.

1917–18
U.S. involvement in World War I.

1941–45
U.S. involvement in World War II.

1964–73
U.S. involvement in Vietnam War.

1861–65
Civil War.

2001
A terrorist attack in which four hijacked airliners crash into New York City's World Trade Center, the Pentagon, and farmland in western Pennsylvania leaves thousands dead or injured.

▼ The city of Savannah, circa 1909.

Festivals and Fun for All

Check web site for exact date and directions.

Annual Blessing of the Fleet, Darien

Every year, Darien hosts a lively festival on the waterfront to celebrate the beginning of shrimping season. Festivities include fireworks, dancing in the street, a fishing rodeo, and a mock pirate ship invasion, as well as the official blessing of the fleet.
www.mcintoshcounty.com

Barnesville Buggy Days, Barnesville

Barnesville is proud to have been the Buggy Capital of the South in the late 1800s.
www.barnesville.org/buggy.html

Big Pig Jig, Vienna

This fun-filled day in honor of barbecue includes a "whole-hog" cooking contest.
www.bigpigjig.com

Columbus Riverfest Weekend, Columbus

A family festival with a children's carnival and cooking contests.
www.historiccolumbus.com

Georgia Apple Festival, Ellijay

Learn about the town of Ellijay, apples, and the mountains of northern Georgia.
www/ngeorgia.com/travel/apple.html

Georgia's International Cherry Blossom Festival, Macon

In the heart of Georgia's fruit-growing district, this festival celebrates spring cherry blossoms.
www.cherry blossom.com

Georgia Mountain Fair, Hiawassee

A twelve-day fair celebrates the mountain lifestyle. Includes country and western music, a midway, dancing, and crafts.
www.georgia-mountain-fair.com

The Georgia National Fair, Perry

A traditional fair featuring contests, midway rides, livestock, food, and even racing pigs.
www.georgianationalfair.com

Georgia State Fair, Macon

A classic state fair with a mix of agricultural exhibits, arts and crafts, and carnival fun.
www.georgia statefair.org

Hahira Honeybee Festival, Hahira

The town of Hahira celebrates the local honey industry with an annual festival that includes not only the crowning of a Honey Queen, a dog show, and races, but also the chance to dunk city officials in dunking booths.
www.hahira.ga.us/honeybee.htm

The Helen Oktoberfest, Helen

A celebration of German food and music in an "alpine" north Georgia setting.
www.helenga.org/visitorinformation/oktoberfest.asp

Indian Summer Festival, Suches

Theater, square dancing, and a quilt show are just some of the possibilities on the site of Georgia's smallest public school.
www.suches.com/events/festival.htm

Mule Roundup Festival, Guysie

Come see what farming was like before tractors. This festival includes bull riding, demonstrations of mule teams, and sausage making, as well as arts and crafts and singing.
www.southfest.com/festivals/guysie.shtml

North Georgia State Fair, Marietta

Contests, concerts, carnival barkers, and Ferris wheels and other rides make this a fun event for the whole family.
www.northgeorgiastatefair.com

▶ A blacksmith demonstrates his trade at Westville.

Prater's Mill Country Fair, Dalton

This tradition-rich festival of music, food, and handicrafts has been delighting people for more than 150 years.
www.pratersmill.org

Southern Heartland Arts Festival, Covington

Master artisans demonstrate historic crafts such as weaving, woodwork, pottery, metalwork, and soap making. More than one hundred artists and craftspeople participate in this free event.
www.shaf.org

Westville, Lumpkin

Westville is a living history museum that recreates village life in western Georgia in the 1850s. Each month the village offers special events at which visitors may travel back in time to observe the daily life of nineteenth-century Georgians.

Winter Storytelling Festival, Atlanta

The Southern Order of Storytellers sponsors this celebration every February. More than thirty storytellers attend to spin their yarns and help young storytellers develop their skills.
www.accessatlanta.com/community/groups/sos/WinterStoryFestival.html

Books

Aaseng, Nathan. *Cherokee Nation v. Georgia.* Farmington Hills, MI: Lucent Books, 2000. Learn more about the tragic forced removal of native peoples from Georgia.

Beatty, Patricia. *Turn Homeward, Hannalee.* New York: William Morrow & Company, 1984. A historical novel based on real-life events in the life of a twelve-year-old Georgia girl separated from her family during the Civil War.

Blackburn, Joyce. *James Edward Oglethorpe.* La Vergne, TN: Consolino and Woodward, 1994. A biography of the Englishman who started the colony of Georgia.

Gibbons, Faye. *Hook Moon Night: Spooky Tales from the Georgia Mountains.* New York: William Morrow Junior Books, 1997. A collection of scary ghost stories told by mountain people of Georgia.

Hammer, Loretta Johnson and Gail Langer Karwoski. *The Tree That Owns Itself: And Other Adventure Tales from Out of the Past.* Atlanta: Peachtree Publishers, 1996. Find out more about the people and places that make Georgia's history unique.

Marsh, Carole. *Georgia History: Surprising Secrets about Our State's Founding Mothers, Fathers and Kids!* Peachtree City, GA: Gallopade, 1997. Discover the ordinary people who have made Georgia extraordinary.

Web Sites

▶ Official state web site
www.state.ga.us/

▶ City of Atlanta Homepage
www.ci.atlanta.ga.us

▶ The Georgia Historical Society
www.georgiahistory.com

▶ About North Georgia
www.ngeorgia.com

INDEX

Note: Page numbers in *italics* refer to maps, illustrations, or photographs.